As someone who grew up in a Christian home but in a denomination that did not celebrate Advent, I have been looking for a biblical guide to worship in anticipation of Christmas since I first heard of the tradition several years back. Finally, Asheritah Ciuciu has written the devotional I had been longing for. *Unwrapping the Names of Jesus* will be a book I will go back to each Christmas season and will be a hallmark of the holiday for years to come.

ERIN ODOM
Author of *More Than Just Making It* and *You Can Stay Home With Your Kids*

The real joy of Christmas comes through the slow unwrapping of God's great gift to us, Jesus Christ. Through beautiful reflections and guided prayers in *Unwrapping the Names of Jesus*, Asheritah facilitates this savoring of Christ. I can't wait to take my children through this book!

CHRISTINE HOOVER
Author of *Searching for Spring: How God Makes All Things Beautiful in Time* and *Messy Beautiful Friendship*

At a time when so many Christians are prone to miss the beauty of the reason we celebrate Christmas, lost in the shuffle of expectations and busyness, Asheritah reminds us with depth and clarity of the One who came to bring the joy of salvation. This is a treat to share with your family during Advent season as you prepare your hearts for Christmas.

MIKE CASTELLI
Lead Pastor, The Chapel in Green

Unwrapping the Names of Jesus is a gift to readers. Through beautiful insight and attention to detail, every devotion deepens our understanding of who Jesus is, and why we celebrate Him not only in the Advent season, but in every season of our lives. This will be a staple during Advent, one we will read year after year. It's a book that invites us to rediscover the depth of Jesus' love for us, through the understanding of His many meaningful names, which all point to the love of God the Father, through His Son, Jesus, Light of the World, Prince of Peace, Lamb of God.

KRIS CAMEALY
Author of *Come, Lord Jesus: The Weight Of Waiting*

I have seen a lot of Advent devotionals, but *Unwrapping the Names of Jesus* is first in the class. Combining substantive theological truth, creative ideas, and personal warmth, Asheritah Ciuciu invites her readers to join her in celebrating the Advent season by focusing their minds and their hearts on Jesus. I heartily recommend it!

DANIEL J. ESTES
Distinguished Professor of Old Testament, Cedarville University

What a gift! Sharing her heart for Jesus in this delightful Advent devotional, Asheritah's *Unwrapping the Names of Jesus* lovingly leads families and individuals to celebrate, worship, and adore Him.

CARMEN BEASLEY
Women's Ministry Director, The Chapel in Green

Unwrapping the Names of Jesus is easy to follow and use, but conveys a depth of truth sure to impact every member of your household. If you are searching for something new to study this Advent, look no further and get this excellent book. Then unwrap the names of Jesus with your family and celebrate together the greatest Christmas gift of all time—our Savior!

MARTY MACHOWSKI
Pastor and author of *Dragon Seed*, (a gospel allegory for teens), *The Ology: Ancient Truths, Ever New*, and other gospel-centered family resources

There is no better time to examine the multifaceted personality of our Savior than in the days leading up to Christmas. Asheritah Ciuciu eloquently pulls back layer after layer of His personhood and His purpose, revealing His character and His kindness, as she unwraps the names of Jesus.

WENDY SPEAKE
Coauthor of *Triggers* and *Life Creative*, writing about faith and family at WendySpeake.com

AN ADVENT
Devotional

UNWRAPPING
the Names
OF
Jesus

ASHERITAH CIUCIU

MOODY PUBLISHERS
CHICAGO

All Scripture quotations, unless otherwise indicated, are taken from the Holy Bible, New International Version®, NIV®. Copyright © 1973, 1978, 1984, 2011 by Biblica, Inc.™ Used by permission of Zondervan. All rights reserved worldwide. www.zondervan.com. The "NIV" and "New International Version" are trademarks registered in the United States Patent and Trademark Office by Biblica, Inc.™

Scripture quotations marked ESV are from The Holy Bible, English Standard Version® (ESV®), copyright © 2001 by Crossway, a publishing ministry of Good News Publishers. Used by permission. All rights reserved.

Emphasis in Scripture has been added.

Published in association with Literary Agent Tawny Johnson of D. C. Jacobson & Associates LLC, 537 SE Ash Street, Suite 203, Portland, OR 97214.

Edited by Connor Sterchi
Interior design: Smartt Guys design
Cover design: Connie Gabbert Design and Illustration
Cover title lettering by Connie Gabbert
Cover photo of wrapped manger copyright © 2017 by Pearl / Lightstock (55051)
All rights reserved.
Author photo: Ashley McComb

Library of Congress Cataloging-in-Publication Data

Names: Ciuciu, Asheritah, author.
Title: Unwrapping the names of Jesus : an Advent devotional / Asheritah
  Ciuciu.
Description: Chicago : Moody Publishers, 2017. | Includes bibliographical
  references.
Identifiers: LCCN 2017027187 (print) | LCCN 2017032880 (ebook) | ISBN
  9780802496300 | ISBN 9780802416728
Subjects: LCSH: Advent--Prayers and devotions. | Jesus Christ--Name--Prayers
  and devotions. | Families--Prayers and devotions.
Classification: LCC BV40 (ebook) | LCC BV40 .C495 2017 (print) | DDC
  242/.332--dc23
LC record available at https://lccn.loc.gov/2017027187

ISBN: 978-0-8024-1672-8

All websites and phone numbers listed herein are accurate at the time of publication but may change in the future or cease to exist. The listing of website references and resources does not imply publisher endorsement of the site's entire contents.

We hope you enjoy this book from Moody Publishers. Our goal is to provide high-quality, thought-provoking books and products that connect truth to your real needs and challenges. For more information on other books and products written and produced from a biblical perspective, go to www.moodypublishers.com or write to:

Moody Publishers
820 N. LaSalle Boulevard
Chicago, IL 60610

7 9 10 8

Printed in the United States of America

*For all those longing to
recapture the joy of Christmas,*

and for my parents,

*who have imprinted on my soul
the love and wonder of Jesus*

CONTENTS

WHY CELEBRATE
ADVENT?

I didn't grow up observing Advent.

In fact, other than carefully placing my boots under the window on St. Nicholas Day (a cherished Romanian tradition) and joining the carolers on Christmas Eve, there wasn't much I looked forward to in the Christmas season. I've always been a terrible gift-buyer, and decorating the tree pretty much ensured a family feud.

For the longest time, Christmas filled me with angst, not just because of childhood memories but also because of the insane pressure we place on ourselves to make the holidays picture perfect. We get so wrapped up in getting everything ready that Christmas morning can sneak up on us, and we end up feeling guilty that we don't have more warm and fuzzy feelings about Jesus on the day we should be celebrating His birth.

THE MOST WONDERFUL TIME OF THE YEAR?

We spend so much of the holiday season creating our own little winter wonderlands: cookies and cards, lights and decorations, carols and get-togethers. But what exactly are we doing to prepare spiritually?

Most Christians agree that Christmas is all about Jesus, yet few of our calendars would reflect that priority. Honestly, there just doesn't seem to be much time with all the extra demands on our schedules. But somewhere along the lines, this "most wonderful time of the year" overwhelms us, making our souls feel both stuffed and empty.

Yes, busyness and consumerism may be partially to blame. But perhaps no one has taught us how to focus our hearts on Jesus during this season. And it's precisely in the cacophony of this holiday busyness that Advent invites us to a simple practice of worship and celebration of Jesus.

EMBRACING AN AGE-OLD TRADITION

I first encountered this idea of Advent as a young college student, and it seemed a bit bizarre at first. *What's with all the candles?* I wondered, sitting back in the pew as I watched a child light purple pillar candles in an evergreen wreath at the front of the church. Besides being a clear fire hazard, this little ritual was accompanied by dry readings of obscure passages that did little to warm my heart. But over the years that followed, Advent seemed to pop up all over the place. Perhaps it was my own heightened awareness, but I was intrigued, so I did a little digging to find out more.

Advent means "coming," from the Latin word *adventus*, and demarks a season of expectantly preparing to celebrate the first coming of Jesus, while eagerly awaiting His second coming to establish His kingdom, even as we celebrate His presence among us through the promised Holy Spirit.

Although it's impossible to pinpoint the exact date the church began observing Advent, the first clear reference to this preparatory period occurred in the sixth century, with some anecdotal mentions as early as AD 380, at the Spanish Council of Saragossa.[1] Various church traditions practice Advent differently, but generally they set aside the four weeks leading up to Christmas to prepare their hearts to celebrate the birth of Jesus Christ.

During the Reformation, some Protestants deemphasized the Christian liturgical calendar in a desire to make a clean break from the Catholic Church. But in so doing, we have lost some of the richness that comes from bridging worship in the twenty-first century to that of the early church. As Philip Meade points out, "Although we are wise to not make our residence in the past, we nevertheless should appreciate and recognize the importance of what the church has been doing for hundreds of years."[2] Insofar as this practice can help us meditate on Scripture and more fully enter the season of Christmas, it is a worthwhile addition to our Christmas traditions, and many evangelical churches are recognizing this as they add Advent practices to their Christmas church programs.

As it's celebrated in the Western church, Advent begins on the fourth Sunday before Christmas and is observed through Christmas

Eve. Observances often include an Advent calendar, Advent daily devotionals, and an Advent wreath, an evergreen wreath containing five candles. Each candle represents a theme and is lit on successive Sundays and Christmas Eve. The themes that correspond to each week also vary by location and denomination, but generally include these variations: *hope* (or promise), *preparation* (or waiting or prophecy), *joy* (or peace), and *love* (or adoration).

Gradually, I warmed up to the idea of Advent and began incorporating it into my own spiritual preparation. One year, as I reflected on the names of Jesus that appear in Christmas carols, I realized that I need to worship Jesus for who He is in the privacy of my home before I can fully celebrate His birth in the company of His congregation. This practice of meditating on a different name each day, while not an Advent tradition per se, taught me to worship Jesus in a way I'd never learned before. Like twirling a brilliant-cut diamond in sunlight, meditating on Jesus' names led me to admire the many facets of His character, each beautiful on its own, but when put together comprising a breathtaking picture of the Son of God made man for us. As the days of Advent passed, I found myself, like David, gazing upon the beauty of the Lord day by day, delighting in Him and dwelling in His presence (Ps. 27:4).

I unwrapped His names one at a time, excitement and anticipation building for the arrival of Christmas Eve. Presents and parties and pastries faded into the background as the drama of Christ's birth took center stage. As I walked into the candlelit service on Christmas Eve, my heart soared at the sight of the manger. This was the moment I had been waiting for. This was what Advent had prepared me for. *This* was the meaning of Christmas. This beautiful, profound, majestic scene of the eternal God entering time and space for you and for me. I sat on the edge of my seat in the pew, eyes glued on the manger, waiting for the service to begin so I could release the praise and adoration that were waiting to burst forth. And in my heart I heard the echoing chorus of believers throughout the ages marveling at God's wondrous gift, joining in with Mary to say, "My soul magnifies the Lord, and my spirit rejoices in God my Savior" (Luke 1:46–47 ESV).

HOW TO USE THIS DEVOTIONAL

We all suffer from soul amnesia, forgetting who God is and what He has done for us from one day to the next. Like you, I too must remind myself each year who Jesus is and why His birth is so miraculous—not because my mind doesn't know but because my heart ceases to be amazed. As the old saying goes, familiarity breeds contempt, and sadly, my own heart loses that sense of wonder. So I wrote this book for you and for me, an offering to help us grow in both our knowledge and love of Jesus. In the words of Jen Wilkin, "The heart cannot love what the mind does not know," so I've endeavored to engage both our hearts and our minds in worship.[3]

I structured this book around the four weeks of Advent (Hope, Preparation, Joy, and Love). Each week begins with an Advent celebration on Sunday, which you can use individually or with your family. You'll find short reflections on the names of Jesus for each weekday, followed by challenges to go deeper, prayers to jump-start your private worship, and additional Scripture references in case you want to study the name further. I've also provided service-oriented ideas and suggestions for activities that can be done during the week or on Saturday to help you apply that week's theme to your Christmas preparations.

I pray this devotional will become your springboard into deeper worship. Whether your devotions take two minutes or two hours is not as important as whether or not your heart is tuned in to the presence of God in that moment and throughout your day. Dive deeper into each name's significance with singing, praying, journaling, or whatever else focuses your attention on Jesus.

Try adopting different body postures before Him, bowing your face to the ground before the Holy One of God, lifting up your palms before the Lord of lords, and dancing with songs of celebration to the King of kings. Engage your senses in worship as well, lighting a scented candle reserved for just your private times of worship with the Great High Priest, praising the Creator as you walk through nature, or fasting from certain foods as you feast on the Bread of Life. Your worship journey will be as rich, deep, and varied as you desire it to be, but know for a fact that you will seek God and find Him when you seek Him with all of your heart (Jer. 29:13). (For more creative ideas on how to worship God and a free printable to keep you inspired, visit www.onethingalone.com/creative-worship.)

GOD DOESN'T MAKE A LIST (NOR DOES HE CHECK IT TWICE)

Any time you spend quieting your heart before God and worshiping Him is time well spent. But be assured of this: God is not going to be disappointed if you miss a day (or a week's) devotional or challenge. Nor is He going to be impressed if you check it off each day.

The purpose of this devotional is not to get more favor with God—Jesus already secured His approval when He took our place on the cross. You are preapproved in Jesus; He invites you to rest in His finished work.[4]

The purpose of this devotional is to help us worship Jesus as we gain a greater sense of awe and wonder at who He is. We prepare our hearts so that when we admire the live nativity scene, when we sit in the candlelight service, and when we wake up Christmas morning, we can join the faithful who have gone before us and sing from the bottom of our hearts, "O come, let us adore Him, Christ the Lord!"

Alongside you in the journey of Christmas joy,

ASHERITAH

YOU AND ME

Father, You know the precious one who is reading this book right now. Before the creation of the world You knew each of us and You made possible a way to redeem us . . . because of Your great love.

Precious Father, I ask that You meet us right where we are this moment. Whether we're climbing the corporate ladder or climbing the Lego-strewn stairs, help us bow low in worship before You. You know our hearts, and You know our desire to be close to You. We claim Your promise that You will draw near to those who draw near to You and You will reward those who diligently seek You with more of Yourself.

As we seek You this holiday season, help us cast aside any impediments that come between us and You. Reassure us of Your unconditional love even when we don't feel like we measure up, especially when we're tempted to place our identity in our to-do list (whether completed or not).

Help us cling to You and be sustained by Your truth as we dig into the names of Jesus. May His names be more than words on a page; may they become a vocabulary of worship as we come into Your presence through Your Son, Jesus.

Fill us with the joy of Your salvation, which we celebrate at Christmastime. Whatever our agenda may hold each day, help us create little pockets of time to meet with You and be refreshed by Your presence. Guide us into Your sanctuary, and don't let us leave until we've met with You.

And at the end of the season, may our love for You continue to grow as we step deeper and deeper into a relationship with You.

Amen.

WEEK ONE

HOPE

*The people walking in darkness have seen
a great light; on those living in the land of
deep darkness a light has dawned.*

ISAIAH 9:2

HOPE

*I*f you are going through this devotional with your family, you can go to unwrappingthenames.com and print out the questions and Scripture readings on separate slips of paper and distribute them among your family members in order to involve everyone. Most of these components are simple enough for even small children to read alone or with help.

OPEN WITH A SIMPLE PRAYER

LIGHT THE FIRST CANDLE ON YOUR ADVENT WREATH

READ THE FOLLOWING VERSE ALOUD:

> "When Jesus spoke again to the people, he said, 'I am the light of the world. Whoever follows me will never walk in darkness, but will have the light of life.'"
> — John 8:12

SOMEONE ASKS:

> Why do we light this candle?

This candle reminds us of the promise that a Messiah would come, bringing peace and love to the world.

Read the following verse aloud:

"The people walking in darkness have seen a great light; on those living in the land of deep darkness a light has dawned." — Isaiah 9:2

Take turns reading through this part of the Christmas story:

Isaiah 9:2–7

Discussion Questions

1. God planned Jesus' arrival thousands of years before it happened. What does that tell us about God?

2. How does Jesus' light in our world give us hope?

3. In what ways can we allow Jesus' light to shine through us?

Sing the following carol together:

Silent Night

As you read the daily devotions this week, light the first candle and thank Jesus for being our Hope.

JESUS

She will give birth to a son, and you are to give him
the name Jesus, because he will save his people from their sins.

MATTHEW 1:21

The name *Jesus* is a transliteration of the Hebrew name *Joshua*, which means "the LORD is salvation." In Bible times, it was not an uncommon name, just like Jesus Himself didn't appear out of the ordinary to those who grew up with Him. Yet His given name holds great significance to who He is and what He did on earth.

In the Old Testament, Joshua led the Israelites into Canaan. He saved the people through courageous leadership, charging into battle upon bloody battle, leading hundreds of thousands into the Promised Land. In contrast to the first Joshua, the second Joshua (Jesus) saved through an epic battle that He fought alone, quietly making the way for His people to enter the Promised Land of God's presence.

Jesus came to save people from their sins. What the first Joshua was powerless to do, the second Joshua was born to accomplish.

During Jesus' lifetime, the Israelites were waiting for a political leader like Joshua who would free them from the yoke of Roman oppression and allow them to live in the land God had promised them, just as their forefathers had been freed from Egyptian slavery and led into Canaan. They wanted a macho man who would reinstate Israel as an autonomous country and make the Romans run in fear.

But Jesus' perspective is always bigger than ours. His gaze was set on the universal dilemma of sin. His battle was one of cosmic proportions, to deliver all who believe in Him from the bondage of soul-deadening sin and welcome us into the family of God.

CHALLENGE

As you enter this season of Advent, what expectations do you have of Jesus? Are you expecting Him to provide finances, heal a loved one, mend a marriage, or fulfill some other request? He very well may . . . but He may not. Regardless of what happens or how He answers, open yourself to His saving touch, and ask Him to show you what He wants to do in your life. Begin the Advent season with an open heart filled with hope because of Jesus our Savior.

PRAYER

Precious Jesus, thank You for coming to save not just Israel but all those who call on You. I often get wrapped up in my own self-righteousness and feel like my salvation is done and over with, but You desire a continual renewal of my heart; You want to save me from my own self-righteousness and transform me into Your image. "Search me, God, and know my heart . . . See if there is any offensive way in me, and lead me in the way everlasting" (Ps. 139:23–24).

FOR FURTHER STUDY

Psalm 139; Isaiah 53; Matthew 21:11; Luke 2:11; Romans 11:26

JESUS IS THE

RESURRECTION AND THE LIFE

I am the resurrection and the life.
The one who believes in me will live, even though they die.

JOHN 11:25

Many people's greatest fear is death. For those who do not believe in God, the thought of dying can be overwhelming, since they don't know what awaits them once they pass away.

Martha and Mary faced the reality of death when their brother, Lazarus, died of a severe illness. He was most likely their sole protector and provider, since neither husbands nor parents are mentioned in their stories. Martha demonstrated her faith in Jesus when she asked Him to resurrect her brother because "God will give you whatever you ask" (John 11:22).

Although Martha properly acknowledged Jesus' relationship with His Father, she failed to understand that Jesus Himself is the resurrection and life. The power of life and death are in Jesus. He spoke the world into existence and breathed life into Adam.[1] He carefully fashions every child in their mother's womb, and several times in the New Testament He filled dead bodies with life again (see "For Further Study" notes below).

Jesus nullified death's hold on His creation when He willingly laid down His own life. He didn't just stop or end death—He overcame it by entering it and annihilating it from within, rising from the dead without requiring anyone's intervention. As Scripture says, "Death has been swallowed up in victory" (1 Cor. 15:54).

Because Jesus rose to life, we who have believed in Him have also been raised to new life with Him. Although we groan with creation under the weight of the current decay death causes in the world, we do not mourn as those without hope. Even in the face of death, whether a cancer diagnosis or an empty place at the holiday table, we embrace the hope of a physical resurrection—ours and that of all who belong to Jesus.

But resurrection is not just a future event. Jesus' words in this passage remind us that resurrection is also a current reality: those who believe in Jesus will ultimately never die. We may experience temporary physical death, but our souls and spirits will continue to live until we receive glorified bodies. We are a resurrected people, and when Jesus returns, we will fully enter His resurrection—body, soul, and spirit. On that day, we will join the chorus of believers who will cheer our resurrected Lord and taunt our former enemy: "Where, O death, is your victory? Where, O death, is your sting?" (1 Cor. 15:55).

Jesus' historical resurrection gives us hope both for today and for the future. Death is defeated in Jesus as He transitions us from temporal life to life eternal. We live the lives of the resurrected.

CHALLENGE

What does it mean to live like the resurrected? What implications does this mindset have on your relationships, job, finances, service, evangelism, and pastimes? Today, pick one of these areas and ask the Holy Spirit to show you how to engage in it as one for whom life is eternal.

PRAYER

Lord, You are the Resurrection and the Life. Our world is still torn by sin and destruction, but we acknowledge Your rule over it and we look forward to the day when there will be no more death, no more sorrow, and no more grieving. In the meantime, help us live out the resurrection of Your Son. May we be an aroma of life to a dying world so that they, too, may enter eternal life with You.

FOR FURTHER STUDY

Psalm 139:13; Luke 7:12–16; 8:41–56; John 11:39–45; Acts 3:15; Romans 8:18–25; Ephesians 2:6; Colossians 3:1; 1 Thessalonians 4:13–16; Revelation 1:18

JESUS IS THE

KING OF KINGS

Where is the one who has been born king of the Jews?
We saw his star when it rose and have come to worship him.

MATTHEW 2:2

At both the beginning and the end of Jesus' physical life, Gentiles proclaimed His kingship. The wise men were the first non-Jews to seek out Jesus, and they came because the cosmos announced His birth in such a glorious manner that they concluded it must be for royalty.

Acknowledging the crime for which Jesus was being crucified, Pilate ordered that a placard be fastened to the cross that read, "Jesus of Nazareth, the King of the Jews." The Jews themselves did not acknowledge Jesus as their King and wanted Pilate to change the sign, but he refused.

Despite their refusal to recognize Jesus' kingship, Jesus *is* King. He came to rule what is rightfully His, both due to His lineage and

His creation-ownership. Matthew dedicates the first part of Jesus' narrative to His genealogy, carefully tracing His lineage to David's royal blood. And Luke outlines Jesus' family tree all the way back to Adam, son of God.

Perhaps the most fitting moment of worship in the New Testament is when Jesus entered Jerusalem victoriously riding on a donkey, the crowds praising God and shouting, "Blessed is the king who comes in the name of the Lord! Peace in heaven and glory in the highest!" (Luke 19:38). Although many in the crowd may not have understood that Jesus' kingdom is not of this world, such praise befits the King of kings, and we who have the benefit of the entire New Testament narrative have ample reason to bow our knees in praise and adoration.

Jesus came first as a humble King, but He will return as a warrior King to claim what is rightfully His. John tells us of the present reality in heaven: "On his robe and on his thigh he has this name written: KING OF KINGS AND LORD OF LORDS" (Rev. 19:16).

The King of Glory is not absent from His kingdom; He is patiently awaiting the time when He will come again to establish His kingdom.

We do not trifle with a weakling, nor do we worship an incompetent wannabe rock star. We worship the King of kings who deserves all honor and glory, and continually receives it from the heavens, creation, angels, and the chorus of His redeemed. Who is this King of Glory? His name is Jesus.

CHALLENGE

The entire universe worships the King of kings—but as humans we often miss out on this privilege. We're often so focused on ourselves that we become prideful, angry, and annoyed with others, especially in the busyness of the holiday season. Today, take your eyes off yourself, and fix your gaze on the King of Glory. Worship Him today.

PRAYER

Most High King, You deserve all my honor and praise. Forgive me for the many times I'm so self-centered that I'm in effect negating Your kingship. What a privilege to worship You. Thank You for the hope within us that we will someday worship You with the angels and the saints who have gone before us in Your glorious throne room. I can't wait!

FOR FURTHER STUDY

Zechariah 9:9; Matthew 2:2; Luke 19:37–44; John 19:15–19; 1 Timothy 1:17, 6:15; Revelation 15:3; 19:16

JESUS IS THE

LIGHT OF THE WORLD

The true light that gives light to everyone
was coming into the world.

JOHN 1:9

Throughout Scripture, darkness often represents evil and false-hood while light represents goodness, truth, and holiness. We naturally fill our homes with light and do our best to avoid dark places where danger may linger in the shadows.

Therefore it comes as no surprise that Jesus assumes this title: "I am the light of the world. Whoever follows me will never walk in darkness, but will have the light of life" (John 8:12). But there is more to that statement than we may first realize.

Jesus illuminates our lives with His brilliance, shining into every nook and cranny. Even the revelation of hidden sin is a gift, like the fortunate early diagnosis of a deadly cancer.[2] He reveals not only our sins but also all that is beautiful surrounding us. He awakens our souls to see the history of redemption and the wonderful works of God all around us. As David says, "In your light we see light" (Ps. 36:9).

Those who believe in Jesus will go to be with Him. At death, those separated from Him will enter darkness and gloom, but we will live in everlasting light and joy with Jesus. This truth gives us hope because no matter how gloomy our lives may be this side of eternity, we know that our future destination is in the kingdom of light, where there will be no night, no darkness, no tears, and no distress.

As Jesus is the Light of the World, so He sends us as lights into the world to illuminate our surroundings with His love and life. Just as the moon reflects the sun's light, so we also reflect Jesus' light, loving our families and our neighbors, serving our church and community with our spiritual gifts, and sharing truth in love in a bleak world.

Jesus, the Light of the World, has placed us in a particular time and place in history, in the lives of specific people, within a specific place to shine brightly for Him, holding forth the Word of life in a million different little ways (Phil. 2:14–16). We carry His light within us, and those who see it cannot help but be attracted to the Light. The True Light desires to give light to everyone; and what's more amazing, He wants to use us, His people, to spread that light.

CHALLENGE

The holiday season is filled with lights: strings of lights on Christmas trees, colorful lights on rooftops, inflatable light-up figures on front lawns, light shows in arboretums, and lighted signs announcing the best sales of the season. It's easy to allow commercial light pollution to drown out the shining light within us. Today, ask the Spirit to shine God's light in your life and help you see God's works all around you; then ask Him to shine through you so that others may see the hope of life eternal and turn to Him.

PRAYER

Oh, great Light of the World, fill up my soul with Your dazzling presence. Thank You for shining Your light in my life. Open my eyes to see the wonderful works of Your hand all around me, and help me do the work You've called me to without complaining or arguing, shining like the stars within this crooked and dark world. Awaken my soul to You, and help me to shine brightly right where You've placed me.

FOR FURTHER STUDY

John 1:4–9, 12:35–36; 1 John 1:5–7

JESUS IS THE
CHRIST (MESSIAH)

When he [King Herod] had called together
all the people's chief priests and teachers of the law,
he asked them where the Messiah was to be born.

MATTHEW 2:4

"C hrist" is the Greek translation of the Hebrew term *Messiah*, which means "the Anointed One."[3] In Old Testament times, anointing signified being set aside for service, particularly as a king or priest. Jesus came not as an anointed one but as *the* Anointed One, both King and Priest, set apart not by any man but by God Himself.

When John the Baptist appeared on the scene, his contemporaries were attracted to his fierce preaching and rugged appearance. Many were convinced he was the Messiah, but he repeatedly told them he was only the forerunner, and called the people to repent in preparation for the Messiah's arrival. The scene was set, and many waited with bated breath to meet the One who would deliver them from all their enemies.

Except Jesus wasn't what they expected. The Jews wanted a military leader who would liberate them from Roman oppression—but Jesus was meek and quiet in spirit. They wanted an established leader, one the rulers of the world would listen to and respect—but Jesus was born in questionable circumstances and possessed no earthly valuables. They wanted a poster child for Jewish superiority —but Jesus hung out with outcasts and upended cultural norms. In short, many Jews were disappointed in Jesus, but the Christ did not come to win a popularity contest.

Jesus is the One on whom all history hinges. All kings and priests before Jesus pointed to Him, prophets spoke of Him, the Magi brought gifts for Him, John the Baptist prepared the people for Him, and the Father anointed Him. And as we move forward, we still look back, counting the years since His coming (the dating system we use today is based on the number of years since Jesus' approximate birth) and circling calendar events celebrating His birth, death, and resurrection.

Jesus was God's answer to Israel's prayers; He was the Messiah, but they rejected Him. "He came to that which was his own, but his own did not receive him. Yet to all who did receive him, to those who believed in his name, he gave the right to become children of God" (John 1:11–12). So gratefully we celebrate Him as the Christ, the Anointed One not just for Israel, but for all humankind who believe in Him.

CHALLENGE

Have you tried to fit Jesus into your idea of who He should be or how He should act? Take time this season to read through the Gospels. Reacquaint yourself with Jesus. Marvel at His miracles. Chuckle at His witty responses to the Pharisees' snide remarks. Weep as His people reject Him and He walks toward Golgotha. Rejoice as the stone is rolled away and the tomb is found empty. Go beyond surface familiarity with the stories and engage with the Anointed One as He is revealed in the pages of Scripture.

PRAYER

Lord, what a privilege to be included in Your family. Forgive me for assuming I know all about You and trying to fit You in a box. Though I can never fathom Your all in all, help me continue learning about Your character. What hope You brought all of us who would have otherwise been lost!

FOR FURTHER STUDY

Job 19:25; Daniel 9:25; Matthew 2:4; 16:16; Luke 9:20; John 1:41

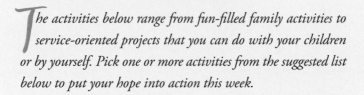

Week One Activities

HOPE IN ACTION

*T*he activities below range from fun-filled family activities to service-oriented projects that you can do with your children or by yourself. Pick one or more activities from the suggested list below to put your hope into action this week.

* **Decorate the Christmas tree together.** As you hang ornaments, reflect and talk about how the evergreen tree symbolizes life in the middle of winter even as Jesus is the Resurrection and the Life. When you glance at the twinkling lights, remember that Jesus is the Light of the World, and He calls us to be shining lights in the darkness. Consider making ornaments to remind you of Jesus' names, or color the printable ones provided at unwrappingthenames.com.

* **Bake cookies** for your mail carrier, garbage collector, or others who regularly care for your needs with little thanks. Write a personal card celebrating the birth of the King of kings, who was born for the high and the lowly.

* **Make Christmas cards for families** in the NICU, whose holiday season is filled with worry and grief. Pray that Jesus, the One who saves, may fill their hearts with hope.

* **Participate in an Angel Tree program** through the Salvation Army or Prison Fellowship, and buy gifts for needy children near you. Find links and more information at unwrappingthenames.com.

* **Help decorate your church for Christmas**, and listen to gospel-rich, Jesus-centered carols that reinforce the reason for the season. Find a playlist at unwrappingthenames.com.

BONUS CONTENT

Go to unwrappingthenames.com to download a free printable activity sheet and other fun resources to celebrate Advent together with your family.

WEEK TWO

PREPARATION

Prepare the way for the LORD.
ISAIAH 40:3

PREPARATION

*I**f you are going through this devotional with your family, you can go to unwrappingthenames.com and print out the questions and Scripture readings on separate slips of paper and distribute them among your family members in order to involve everyone. Most of these components are simple enough for even small children to read alone or with help.*

OPEN WITH A SIMPLE PRAYER

LIGHT THE FIRST TWO CANDLES ON YOUR ADVENT WREATH

READ THE FOLLOWING VERSE ALOUD:

> "In him [Jesus] was life, and that life was the light of all mankind. The light shines in the darkness, and the darkness has not overcome it." — John 1:4–5

SOMEONE ASKS:

> Why do we light the second candle?

SOMEONE RESPONDS:

> The second candle reminds us that the prophets waited for a Messiah to come and save the people.

> "A voice of one calling: 'In the wilderness prepare the
> way for the LORD; make straight in the desert a highway
> for our God. Every valley shall be raised up, every
> mountain and hill made low; the rough ground shall
> become level, the rugged places a plain. And the glory
> of the LORD will be revealed, and all people will see it
> together. For the mouth of the LORD has spoken.'"
> — Isaiah 40:3–5

TAKE TURNS READING THROUGH THIS PART OF THE CHRISTMAS STORY:

Luke 1:26–38

DISCUSSION QUESTIONS

1. God wanted His people to be ready for the coming
   Messiah, so He sent prophets throughout history
   to remind them to prepare their hearts. He also sent
   John the Baptist to prepare the people for Jesus'
   coming. What does this tell us about God?

2. How can we prepare our hearts to celebrate the birth
   of Jesus?

SING THE FOLLOWING CAROL TOGETHER:

O Come, O Come, Emmanuel

*As you read the daily devotions this week, light the first two candles
and thank Jesus for being the Answer to our preparation.*

JESUS IS THE

WORD OF GOD

In the beginning was the Word,
and the Word was with God,
and the Word was God.

JOHN 1:1

The English dictionary defines *word* as a distinct meaningful element of speech used to communicate.[1] But the Greek audience John was writing to would have understood the nuances of that term to include both "the outward form by which the inward thought is expressed and the inward thought itself."[2] This use of the term *logos* for Jesus as the Word of God has several implications:

Jesus is God's creative Word who spoke everything into existence: the beautiful flowers, majestic mountains, brilliant northern lights, fascinating animals, and breathtaking sunsets. God's creation speaks to us His eternal power and divine nature because it was fashioned by the Creative Word Himself.

Jesus is God's communicative Word as well because Jesus is God in the flesh. In the past, God used prophets to speak to His people, sharing His thoughts and intentions with a select few, who then spread His message to the masses. But in Jesus, God's Word became readily available to whoever was willing to listen. Jesus is the full revelation and intelligent communication of God.

Lastly, Jesus is God's final Word. He fulfills Old Testament prophesies that point to Him and not only sets in motion but finishes God's redemptive plan for His people. On the cross, bearing the sins of all those who believed and would believe in Him, Jesus said these marvelous words: "It is finished" (John 19:30). Nothing more needs to be added or changed in order for people to have a relationship with God, and nothing in history will change the finality of Jesus' work on the cross. Jesus is all we need.

Without Jesus, our communication from God would have been indirect, impersonal, and distant. In Jesus, we have the very Word of God—the most direct, personal, meaningful communication God could ever give us—available to everyone who seeks Him.

Jesus is the Word of God made accessible to old and young, schooled and illiterate, Jew and Gentile, past and present. And in this Word-become-flesh, we see the greatest manifestation of God's love.

CHALLENGE

When we think of "spending time in the Word," we often think of merely reading the Bible. And while studying Scripture is important, it should always drive us to a deeper relationship with Jesus. Today, let your time in the Word drive you to spend time with the Word. Talk to Him. Invite Him to speak into your life right now. And then listen to the Word.

PRAYER

Father, thank You for giving us Your Word, Jesus, through whom we can learn more about You. Forgive me for neglecting Him, as if He's hidden in the pages of history instead of alive and eager to reveal You. Quiet my heart and open my soul to listen to Him.

FOR FURTHER STUDY

Genesis 1:3–31; John 1:1, 12:49; Romans 1:20; Revelation 19:13

JESUS IS THE

TRUTH

I am the way and the truth and the life.
No one comes to the Father except through me.

JOHN 14:6

Jesus made many "I am" statements, but one of the most intriguing is when He calls Himself the Truth.

Think about it: Satan is called "the father of lies" (John 8:44). He specializes in twisting truth and casting a shadow on God's character. (To see him in action, just read Genesis 3 or Luke 4:1–13.) For Satan, to spew lies is in keeping with his character. We would expect nothing less of him.

But Jesus is not just the opposite of the devil, just as truth is not merely the absence of a lie. Truth is the construct that defines reality. It stands in stark contrast to a lie because lies cannot exist without something to twist and oppose. Truth, in contrast, exists on its own. It needs nothing external to prop it up; it needs no other affirmation.

Jesus is God's truth. All He says is true and His very life demonstrates a life lived in singleness of mind and truth. As Randy Alcorn explains, He is "the source of all truth, the embodiment of truth, and therefore the reference point for evaluating all truth-claims."[3] We, however, are tempted to live compartmentalized lives, the persona we adopt in church on Sunday morning remarkably different than the one in the boardroom Tuesday afternoon or the one watching movies Friday night. Our enemy whispers that no one's watching, no one cares, no one's keeping track, his lies slithering around our necks like a noose. And just as he did in the garden of Eden, he tempts us to question God's goodness, His presence, His provision, and His love for us, sending us into a tailspin, wondering what's really real.

But whereas we're ambushed by the enemy's lies, Jesus stands grounded in the reality that is truth. He defines it, He lives it, and He calls us to experience the freedom that comes from walking in Him, for "you will know the truth, and the truth will set you free" (John 8:32). Jesus, the Truth, frees us from the chains of falsehood to discover the fullness of life that comes when His presence fills our lives.

When we fix our gaze on Jesus, we learn to see life through the prism of reality, what is really true, instead of through the tinted glasses that our enemy would have us wear.

In fact, when Jesus faced Pilate on the day of His death, He made this aspect of His character very clear: "The reason I was born and came into the world is to testify to the truth. Everyone on the side of truth listens to me." Pilate responded with an age-old question that's ever-so-relevant today: "What is truth?" (John 18:37). Face-to-face with truth Himself, Pilate was too wrapped up in his own view of the world to acknowledge Him.

The only way to recognize lies is to be intimately acquainted with truth, much like investigators recognize counterfeit currency by studying the real thing. We must fill our hearts and minds with the Truth, bathing all of life in His presence, so that we immediately recognize the enemy's lies when he tries to deceive us. It's Jesus, the Truth, who sets us free.

CHALLENGE

What lies about God, yourself, relationships, emotions, and life are you battling today? Write them on an index card, and take a few moments to find truth in Scripture on that topic (you can use a concordance online or at the back of your Bible). Write those verses on the back of the index card and then spend time with the Truth. Ask Him to transform the way you view that area of your life so that you can walk in the freedom of the truth.

PRAYER

Jesus, You are the Truth that sets us free. So often I let the enemy whisper lies into my heart and I actually believe them. Help me to fill my life with You and with Your words so that I can recognize lies when I see them. Fill me to overflowing with Your truth so that Your words spill out into the lives of those around me, bringing them hope, joy, and freedom in You.

FOR FURTHER STUDY

John 8:32; 17:17; 3 John 1:3

JESUS IS THE

LION OF JUDAH

Then one of the elders said to me,
"Do not weep! See, the Lion of the tribe of Judah,
the Root of David, has triumphed."

REVELATION 5:5

In *The Lion, the Witch, and the Wardrobe*, C. S. Lewis delights children and adults with an imaginative allegory presenting gospel truths. Aslan, the lion who rules Narnia, exemplifies many of the characteristics of Jesus, particularly evident when Lucy asks if Aslan is safe.

"Safe?" said Mr. Beaver; "don't you hear what Mrs. Beaver tells you? Who said anything about safe? 'Course he isn't safe. But he's good. He's the King, I tell you."[4]

In popular portrayals of Jesus, it's common to picture Him as a humble and gentle Caucasian man with long-flowing hair that gently frames His face as He meekly knocks on a wooden door.

But Scripture gives us a much richer portrayal that cannot be described with any one image or metaphor.

Though Jesus humbled Himself as a servant to all, He is not a pushover. Do not confuse His humility with weakness. Humility can best be understood as power under control. From being birthed in a manger to being hung on a cross, Jesus' valor lies exactly in the fact that He restrained His glorious might when He could have obliterated all who stood against Him.

Jesus is fierce. Like a young lion, His raw power makes His enemies scatter. We see glimpses of this when He cleared the temple of money changers and merchants, expressing His righteous indignation by turning over tables and sending coins flying. The Lion of the Tribe of Judah has already won the battle, and when He returns to settle accounts with the kingdom of darkness, He will unleash His fury against all His enemies (Isa. 34:1–8). All who stand against Him will fall, but all who are gathered behind Him will rest in safety.[5]

Jesus also exhibits the sovereign power and position of a great lion towering above his pride. We may appreciate many men and women throughout history for their work and dedication to the kingdom, but only One is worthy of our worship and adoration. Only One is the King of kings, royal, wise, and seated above all, the name that is above all other names (Phil. 2:9–11).

The title "Lion of Judah" reminds us not only of Jesus' valor and sovereignty, but also His faithfulness. From Genesis to Revelation, the Bible is filled with allusions to the Lion of Judah, pointing toward the one who would come to rule the nation, first David and later Jesus, David's descendant. And God always keeps His promises. Although we await the fulfillment of some prophesies, His faithfulness in the past reassures us of His trustworthiness both today and in the future.

Jesus is the triumphant Lion of Judah. And though His enemies scatter in fear, we know He is good. His awe-inspiring strength comforts us even as it reminds us to posture our hearts in humble adoration.

CHALLENGE

Have you adopted our culture's view of Jesus as "safe"? Today, meditate on His power and glory as the Lion of Judah. Ask Him to awaken you to the reality of His grandeur and respond in humble worship.

PRAYER

Jesus, You are the Lion of Judah, who sits enthroned, making Your enemies Your footstool. Teach my soul once more how awesome and majestic is Your name. And help me respond with humility, praise, and adoration.

FOR FURTHER STUDY

Genesis 49:8–12; Psalm 2:10–12; Hosea 5:14; Matthew 21:12–13; Revelation 5:1–14

JESUS IS THE

HOLY ONE OF GOD

We have come to believe and to know that
you are the Holy One of God.

JOHN 6:69

There is something about holiness that scares us, and rightfully so. In his description of heaven, Isaiah writes that as the seraphim called out "Holy, holy, holy is the LORD Almighty; the whole earth is full of his glory," the whole temple shook and filled with smoke (Isa. 6:3). On the throne sat the LORD, the preincarnate Son of God, surrounded by seraphim who covered their faces and feet in appropriate humility. At the sight of this heavenly scene, Isaiah fell to the ground, filled with terror over his own uncleanness.

In fact, throughout the Old Testament God warns the Israelites not to enter His holy presence because their sinfulness would lead to certain death. Only the high priest could enter the Holy of Holies, and that only after going through a painstaking process to purify himself from any sin, known or unknown (Ex. 19:21–22).

A holy God requires absolute holiness; anything less leads to death.

To be holy is to be set apart, to be different from everything else, to be free from any blemish or hint of sin. In the entire history of humanity, no one has been holy . . . except Jesus. Jesus' holiness sets Him apart from everyone else. He is morally perfect. He has never sinned. He has never tempted anyone else to sin. He Himself has defeated sin. The writer of Hebrews refers to Him as "holy, innocent, unstained, separated from sinners" (7:26 ESV).

That's why the self-righteous religious rulers of the day hated Him: they stood condemned in His presence. And that's why the demons trembled before Him: they feared for their very existence.[6]

But we do not have to fear. Jesus' holiness does not threaten those who love Him. In fact, it's His very holiness that gives us reason to hope. Because Jesus is the Holy One of God, He alone is able to clothe us with divine righteousness that we would not have on our own. No one else could do what Jesus has done for us.

We do not have to draw back from God or fear entering His presence, precisely because Jesus' sacrifice pays the penalty of our sins and cleanses us from our unrighteousness. He who knew no sin became sin so that we might become the righteousness of God (2 Cor. 5:21). When God looks at us, He sees us as holy and righteous because of Jesus. We are already positionally holy before God even as we continue to grow practically in this holiness day by day, through the power of His Holy Spirit in us.

CHALLENGE

Each time we confess our sins and yield an area of our lives to Jesus' control, we grow a little more in His holy likeness. Today, take a few moments to confess the sins that have accumulated in your soul; then thank Jesus for being faithful to forgive you your sins and cleanse you from all unrighteousness. Rejoice in the holiness Jesus confers upon you, and walk in His holiness today.

PRAYER

Jesus, You are the Holy One of God. But You are also close to everyone who calls on You. What can I do but praise You? Like the angels standing before Your throne, I too join them in singing, "Holy, holy, holy is the Lord God Almighty, who was, and is, and is to come!" (Rev. 4:8). Help me to see today's minor annoyances and problems as insignificant in light of Your eternal holiness. Make my every word and action today an act of worship to You.

FOR FURTHER STUDY

Leviticus 9–10; Psalm 16:10–11; Isaiah 41:14; Mark 1:24; John 6:69; Acts 3:14; 1 Peter 1:19; 2:22; 1 John 3:5

JESUS IS THE

LORD OF LORDS

God, the blessed and only Ruler, the King of kings and
the Lord of lords, who alone is immortal and who lives
in unapproachable light, whom no one has seen or can see.
To him be honor and might forever.

1 TIMOTHY 6:15–16

Though lords still exist today in some parts of the world, the term is used mostly as an honorary badge, so it's easy to forget what the term even means. Throughout history, lords were rulers who had authority, control, or power over others. In feudal societies lords passed their title from father to son, and their subjects were expected to give immediate and full obedience to whatever their lord ordered.

But Jesus is not just a lord. He is the Lord. He is the Lord of lords, the Lord of righteousness, and the Lord of glory. As such, He is more than just one of a few who rule; He is the Ruler of those who rule.

Many people who came to Jesus addressed Him as Lord, but did not place themselves under His rule. To call Jesus "Lord" but to allow Him no influence over our daily decisions is to make a masquerade of our spiritual lives. He is not our Lord if He does not have supreme authority to direct our actions, from the big-picture decisions of life to the minute daily details. We cannot bring only parts of our lives into submission to our Lord.

Jesus deserves to rule our lives by virtue of who He is, but in this life, He does not impose that lordship on us. For now, it is our choice to willingly acknowledge Him, but one day "every knee should bow . . . and every tongue acknowledge that Jesus Christ is Lord, to the glory of God the Father" (Phil. 2:10–11).

When we submit to His lordship in our lives, we can rest assured that we are in good hands. Unlike earthly lords who are motivated by greed and pride, our Lord is motivated by goodness and righteousness. Our best interests are intimately woven into His, so when we act on what He tells us to do, we inevitably do what will bring us into a more abundant life of joy.

CHALLENGE

Consider what parts of your life you've been withholding from Jesus' lordship. Does He have complete control of your time, finances, schedule, relationships, career, and dreams? Spend some time today renewing your allegiance to your Lord. Bow your knees in worship to Him, and when He instructs you to do something, trust Him and obey immediately.

PRAYER

Lord, too often I've called You "Lord" from my lips, only to selfishly guard the ruling of my own life. Teach me to humble myself before You, to bow my heart, my knees, and my will to You. I give You all I have; it is Yours. Do with me as You will.

FOR FURTHER STUDY

Jeremiah 23:6; Acts 10:36; 1 Corinthians 2:8; 1 Timothy 6:15

he activities below range from fun-filled family activities to service-oriented projects that you can do with your children or by yourself. Pick one or more activities from the suggested list below to put your preparation into action this week.

* **Make snowflakes** by cutting out patterns on simple white paper. On one side, write out prayer requests from your family, your community, or around the world. On the other side, write out a Bible verse that speaks to each request. Then hang them around your living room, pausing to pray as you tape each one up, and continuing to pray whenever you walk through your winter wonderland.

* **Act out the nativity story**, either as a play, a musical, or a puppet show. If you have little ones, you could practice it several times over the course of Advent, and then stage an event for the grandparents and extended family. Even if you don't have children at home, consider acting out the story anyway—little details come alive when we place ourselves in the scene.

* **Sing gospel-centered Christmas carols** that center your heart and attention on Jesus. Find an old hymnal you can thumb through, or use the Advent playlist I've compiled for you at unwrappingthenames.com.

* **Memorize a Christmas verse** or a verse that features a name of Jesus that has stood out to you this week. Write it out on a piece of paper and carry it with you, or find made-for-you memory cards at unwrappingthenames.com.

* **Gift handmade nativity ornaments**. You could draw a little nativity scene, or a star, or write out a name of Jesus. Or, if you're more artistic, draw a lion, a lamb, a shepherd, or a vine. You could make an entire set of coordinating ornaments based on the names of Jesus. (Or download coloring ornaments at unwrappingthenames.com.)

* **Write a letter to Jesus**, responding to what you've learned about Him this week. Thank Him for who He is, confess any sins that have accumulated in your life, and ask Him to give you a deeper love and understanding of Him. Then surrender any area of your life that is hurting this Christmas season, and ask Him to fill you with His joy.

* **Play "traveling wise men" with your nativity set.** Set up the scene as you normally would, but instead of placing the wise men with the rest of the figurines, place them in the farthest corner of the house. Each day, move them closer and closer to the nativity set, until they finally reach the baby Jesus.

BONUS CONTENT

Go to unwrappingthenames.com to download a free printable activity sheet and other fun resources to celebrate Advent together with your family.

WEEK THREE

JOY

I bring you good news that will cause
great joy for all the people.

LUKE 2:10

JOY

If you are going through this devotional with your family, you can go to unwrappingthenames.com and print out the questions and Scripture readings on separate slips of paper and distribute them among your family members in order to involve everyone. Most of these components are simple enough for even small children to read alone or with help.

OPEN IN PRAYER

LIGHT THE FIRST THREE CANDLES ON YOUR ADVENT WREATH

READ THE FOLLOWING VERSE ALOUD:

> "Light shines on the righteous and joy on the upright in heart. Rejoice in the LORD, you who are righteous, and praise his holy name." — Psalm 97:11–12

SOMEONE ASKS:

> Why do we light the third candle?

SOMEONE RESPONDS:

> The third candle reminds us that Jesus' birth brings joy to all who believe in Him, so we join all of creation in celebrating Him.

"When they saw the star, they were overjoyed. On coming to the house, they saw the child with his mother Mary, and they bowed down and worshiped him."
— Matthew 2:10–11a

TAKE TURNS READING THROUGH THIS PART OF THE CHRISTMAS STORY:

Luke 2:1–7

DISCUSSION QUESTIONS

1. When Jesus was born, God sent angels to announce Jesus' birth and also a star to celebrate. The wise men saw the star and traveled a long way to find and worship Jesus. What do these acts tell us about God?

2. How does the birth of Jesus give us joy?

3. In what ways can we spread the joy of Christmas to others?

SING THE FOLLOWING CAROL TOGETHER:

Joy to the World

As you read your daily devotions this week, light three candles and thank Jesus for being our Joy.

JESUS IS THE

GREAT HIGH PRIEST

Therefore, since we have a great high priest
who has ascended into heaven, Jesus the Son of God,
let us hold firmly to the faith we profess.

HEBREWS 4:14

The most prestigious spiritual leader in Israel was the high priest. Of all the priests and rulers in the nation, he was the only one who could enter the Holy of Holies once a year on the Day of Atonement to offer sacrifices for the sins of the people.[1]

After ceremonial cleansing for his own sins, he would go behind the thick veil that separated the Holy Place from the Holy of Holies. There he would offer the blood of a goat on the golden mercy seat that sat atop the Ark of the Covenant, so that the sins of Israel would be covered for another year.

The old priesthood and system of sacrifices was not meant to last forever. God gave them to Moses and the Israelites to foreshadow their fulfillment in Jesus. They had to repeat sacrifices every year, but Jesus' death on the cross made final atonement for our sins and abolished the system once and for all.

Just as the Aaronic high priests would disappear from the people's view when they entered the Holy of Holies, so Jesus passed through the heavens into the sanctuary of God. He is the One to hear our prayers because He has entered the Holy of Holies in heaven.[2]

As the writer of Hebrews explains, there were many high priests throughout history "since death prevented them from continuing in office; but because Jesus lives forever, he has a permanent priesthood" (7:23–24). He remains to this day the enduring High Priest who is alive and able to fulfill that role.

In heaven, Jesus sits on the great throne of grace, ready to hear our prayers and assist us in our time of need; He sympathizes with our weaknesses because He Himself was tempted in every way, just as we are, yet without sin (Heb. 4:15–16). Jesus is not aloof and prideful but rather concerned and available. This comforting truth invites us to approach the throne of grace with confidence.

Because Jesus is our High Priest, we no longer need anyone else to intercede between us and God. We have direct access to the Father through Jesus, and He stands ready and willing to help us in our time of need.

CHALLENGE

What a privilege to have direct access to God! It might seem strange to picture the Old Testament sacrifices, especially since many of us recoil from the sight of blood and the fear of pathogens. But understanding the priests' role in offering sacrifices helps us rejoice in the finished work of Jesus. So approach the throne of grace confidently today and pour out your heart to God. You will not be turned away.

PRAYER

Dear Jesus, I can't even fathom what a big deal this is. You freed us of the requirements of purification, rituals, sacrifices, and law. Through Your death on the cross, You tore the curtain that separated us from the presence of God, and now we can come directly to You, without any other mediator. Forgive me for neglecting this privilege so often. Rekindle in me a desire to spend time in Your presence and to live my life in the daily realities of Your throne room.

FOR FURTHER STUDY

Leviticus 16:1–34; 1 Timothy 2:5; Hebrews 4:14–16; 6:19–7:28; 1 John 2:1

JESUS IS THE

ALPHA AND OMEGA

"I am the Alpha and the Omega," says the Lord God,
"who is, and who was, and who is to come, the Almighty."

REVELATION 1:8

For those who are unfamiliar with the Greek alphabet, this name may not mean much at first. But simply saying "Alpha and Omega" means "A to Z" wouldn't do it justice.

Alpha and Omega are the first and last letters of the Greek alphabet and represent the entirety of not just letters but all knowledge, all existence, and all time. From beginning to end, Jesus was, is, and will be, and all things live, move, and have their being in Him (Acts 17:28). There is nothing outside the realm of His presence. He sovereignly rules over all existence. Through Him all things were created that will be, and in Him all things hold together (Col. 1:16–17).

But Jesus is not only the beginning and end of all creation, He is also the author and finisher of our faith. He experienced the full range of human life alongside us, yet without sin. From His birth in a humble stable to being ostracized by His own community to hanging on a cross like a criminal, Jesus lived the life of faith, entrusting Himself to His Father and walking in obedience. And when He breathed His last breath, He declared, "It is finished." The work of justification had its beginning and its end in Jesus.

Jesus did all this looking at His current circumstances through the eyes of faith, knowing "the joy set before him" (Heb. 12:2). For Jesus, that joy was knowing that He would be resurrected in glory and spend eternity with His bride, the church, which He came to save. We can take comfort in our Alpha and Omega, knowing that whatever we experience in this journey of faith, we are not alone: Jesus has gone before us, He welcomed us into this journey, and He will see us safely to the end.

CHALLENGE

Faith is "confidence in what we hope for and assurance about what we do not see" (Heb. 11:1), trusting God's character regardless of what our life's circumstances look like. In what area of your life do you need to trust the Author and Perfector of your faith? Surrender it to Him today, asking Him to continue to work faith in that area of your life.

PRAYER

Jesus, thank You for going before me. Nothing is unknown to You, even when I wonder how bills will get paid and how life is going to work out. You endured so much more in Your life, yet You did it with joy. Help me to trust You not just at the beginning of my journey, but every day until the very end.

FOR FURTHER STUDY

John 1:3; 19:30; Hebrews 5:9; 12:2; 13:8; Revelation 1:8, 17

JESUS IS THE

TRUE VINE

I am the true vine, and my Father is the gardener . . .
you are the branches.

JOHN 15:1, 5A

When I was growing up, my father was an amateur viticulturist, passionately tending to the grapevines in our backyard. I quickly bored of the tedious work, but he would spend hours in his little vineyard, pruning, twisting, tying, digging, watering—doing all he could to ensure a full harvest come autumn.

Throughout the Old Testament, the vine was used as a symbol of Israel, often to show how she was lacking in some way. God carefully tended His vine, protecting it from harsh elements and creating an environment for it to flourish, yet Israel rebelled. God was just to judge her harshly, but He graciously provided another Vine.

In contrast to Israel, Jesus is the True Vine. He is the faithful One who fulfills all that Israel failed to do: whereas she was wild and rebellious, He was submissive and obedient; while she yielded bad fruit, He produced good fruit in keeping with righteousness. He was in every way the epitome of all God called His people to do, and He calls us to union with Him so that we may also produce good fruit.

Left to ourselves, we cannot produce good fruit any more than Israel remained faithful; we are subject to the same weaknesses and sin-impulses as they were thousands of years ago. By ourselves, we would go the way of rebellious Israel. So God snipped our branch from the wild vine, grafted us into His family through Jesus, and tenderly creates the opportune environment for us to flourish.

If you wonder about your spiritual fruitfulness, Jesus' last conversation with His disciples before His death offers a beautiful opportunity for prayerful reflection: "I am the vine; you are the branches. Whoever abides in me and I in him, he it is that bears much fruit, for apart from me you can do nothing" (John 15:5 ESV). These were the very men who in a few hours would abandon their Teacher, but afterwards repented and went on to spread the good news of Jesus throughout the world. So there is hope for any one of us who has walked away but returns with a repentant heart; the Vinedresser will prune us to produce outward fruit that demonstrates inner transformation.

Surprisingly, Jesus does not call us to work hard to be more fruitful; rather, He calls us to abide in Him, to wait on Him. Fruit will naturally follow for those who remain connected to Him, because

His Spirit is the One who produces the fruit (Gal. 5:22–25). We belong not because of what we do but because of who He is. He is the Vine. We are the branches, and He will bear fruit through us as we remain in Him.

As the True Vine, Jesus both fulfills Old Testament prophecy and makes possible our inclusion in God's family. He sustains us, connecting us with the nourishment we need to bear fruit. He pulses out healing salve to bind our wounds when the Gardener prunes us to be more fruitful. He supports us when the weight we carry seems too much to bear.

Jesus is the reason we're part of the Vine. Apart from Him, we can do nothing. In Him, we can bear much fruit for His kingdom. We need only to abide, and He will do the rest.

CHALLENGE

Recognizing our destructive bent toward self-reliance, Jesus urges His followers to "remain in me" five times in only eight verses. Today, read John 15:1–8 and reflect on the invitation to savor a close connection to the True Vine. Are you as close as He invites you to be? Take a few moments to rest before God. Become mindful of His presence both in deep moments of worship and in the dynamic movements of your daily life. Throughout the day, recognize His life pulsing through you and energizing you for His work even as you learn to rest in Him.

PRAYER

My Vine, thank You for being faithful when I—and the rest of the world—was unfaithful. What we were unable to do, You did perfectly, and You invite us into sweet fellowship with You so that we may learn from You and bear much fruit through the Spirit. Forgive me for trying to produce good works on my own; help me to rely on You and to rejoice in my connection to You.

FOR FURTHER STUDY

Psalm 80:8–16; Isaiah 5:1–7

JESUS IS THE

PRINCE OF PEACE

For to us a child is born, to us a son is given. . . .
And he will be called . . . Prince of Peace. Of the greatness
of his government and peace there will be no end.

ISAIAH 9:6–7A

During His time on earth, Jesus restored peace everywhere He went. He calmed tumultuous storms; He brought healing to the sick; He raised the dead to life; He forgave sinners their sins.

Isaiah prophetically calls the coming Messiah the "Prince of Peace" (Isa. 9:6), and the angels announcing the birth of Jesus declare "on earth peace to those on whom his favor rests" (Luke 2:14).

Jesus came to restore not just peace as we understand a cessation of hostility, but a rich, full, abiding harmony of life. His first coming began this process of restoring peace between us and God; His second coming will bring wholeness as He intended His creation to be when He first set the universe in motion.

In contrast to human history filled with war, gloom, and despair, the reign of Jesus will be marked by flourishing peace, wholeness, and delight. Isaiah 9 describes the shift from gloom and darkness to the Messianic Age, and Malachi describes a time when the "the sun of righteousness shall rise with healing in its wings" (Mal. 4:2 ESV). Jesus' rule will restore well-being to individuals and to society as a whole when He brings worldwide peace in His future kingdom on the new earth.

But Jesus' reign of peace is not reserved for His future kingdom; it begins here and now for all those who follow Him. The Prince of Peace brings us peace with God, the end of spiritual enmity and striving to secure God's favor through our good works, as well as peace of mind and heart, a state of being at rest despite difficult circumstances because we know that God is in control. In fact, the very night Jesus was betrayed, in His last teaching moments with His disciples, Jesus promised them peace, not as the world offers it, but as only He can give give (John 14:27). No matter what would happen, they could rest and enjoy sweet fellowship with God, which would then create ripple effects in their relationships with the world around them.

We live the present reality of God's kingdom, pushing back the kingdom of darkness and bringing to fruition the peace of Jesus. Just as He is the Prince of Peace, so He calls us to be makers of peace all around us (Matt. 5:9). Though the world may be caught up in anxiety and worry, we can rest securely in the knowledge that Jesus is making all things right, and we can participate with Him in bringing peace to a broken world as we look forward to the future kingdom of peace.

CHALLENGE

The holiday season is rife with opportunities to bicker and worry. Family get-togethers can be filled with tension, as jealousy and old wounds often shatter Christmas peace. Think ahead to your social commitments and write down the names of people who cause unrest in your heart. Spend time with Jesus today, asking for His direction in those relationships and committing yourself to being an ambassador of peace this holiday season.

PRAYER

What a beautiful picture You paint for us, Jesus! I can't wait for Your reign to begin and for all the ugliness of sin to disappear. But in the here and now, fill me with Your peace and help me to bring peace in all my interactions. Where there is worry, bring a reassurance of Your provision. Where there is strife, bring to mind Your humility. Where there is bickering, bring to our hearts Your love. Be our peace.

FOR FURTHER STUDY

Judges 6:20–24; Isaiah 8:21–9:7; 11:1–9; Luke 2:14; Acts 3:15; Romans 5:1; Ephesians 2:13–18; Philippians 4:7; Revelation 1:4

JESUS IS THE

BREAD OF LIFE

*Then Jesus declared, "I am the bread of life.
Whoever comes to me will never go hungry,
and whoever believes in me will never be thirsty."*

JOHN 6:35

In the ancient Middle East, bread was a staple part of people's diet. It was the most reliable source of energy for the body and was readily available with little preparation. For the Israelites in particular, bread was considered a special food because of its religious connotations. In the tabernacle and later the temple, there was a table of showbread in the Holy Place that symbolized God's desire to fellowship with His people as well as the bit of manna that was hidden in the Ark of the Covenant in the Holy of Holies as a symbol of God's provision.

When Jesus used the phrases "bread of life" and "bread . . . from heaven," His listeners would have immediately thought of the story of manna. God gave manna to the traveling Israelites in the wilderness to save them from certain death by starvation. In a similar way, God gave Jesus into the world to save us from certain death by separation from Him.

But Jesus wasn't simply drawing a parallel to Moses. He taught that the Bread of Life is greater than the manna their ancestors received under Moses. In fact, His declaration came shortly after the feeding of the five thousand, a miracle that became an object lesson about the greatness of Jesus over Moses. The manna God provided through Moses satisfied only temporarily. The manna Jesus was offering, His very life, satisfies eternally.

Jesus offers Himself to all who believe in Him, an invitation to fellowship that isn't restricted to priests as the showbread was but is open to all—just as Jesus Himself ate with tax collectors, prostitutes, and sinners. And in the beautiful picture of the Last Supper, we're reminded that Jesus' broken body secures our place at God's table. As a morsel of bread becomes part of our bodies and gives us energy, so Jesus becomes part of us when we believe in Him and opens access to fellowship with God. He satisfies every longing and desire with Himself: "In your presence there is fullness of joy; at your right hand there are pleasures forevermore" (Ps. 16:11 ESV). The Bread of Life invites us to feast on Him.

CHALLENGE

Many people try to fill the void in their lives with more stuff—more shopping, more money, more friends, more food—but they're always left wanting more. As Christmas draws near, examine your heart and your desires. Do you crave more stuff, or do you crave more of Jesus? Ask Him to give you a hunger for more of Him.

PRAYER

Jesus, You are everything I've ever wanted. But how often I turn to other things to satisfy the desires of my soul. Forgive me for replacing You with idols in my life. Only You can satisfy. Teach me to hunger for You and feast on You. May You be my heart's chief desire.

FOR FURTHER STUDY

Leviticus 24:5–9; Matthew 5:6; John 6:25–27; 14:6

Week Three Activities

*T*he activities below range from fun-filled family activities to service-oriented projects that you can do with your children or by yourself. Pick one or more activities from the suggested list below to put your joy into action this week.

* **Go caroling in your neighborhood** to bring the joy of Jesus' birth to your surrounding community. You can also visit nursing homes, police and fire stations, hospitals, and homeless shelters. This doesn't have to be long or complicated—just a few gospel-centered songs on joy-filled lips can make a world of a difference in someone's life.

* **Make snow angels** outside or use watercolors to paint angels inside. Reflect on the angels' role in the nativity story, declaring the birth of the Prince of Peace (Luke 2:14).

* **Ask grandparents about what Christmas was like when they were kids**. Share family memories together, and consider how the joy of Jesus' birth—the Alpha and Omega—has been a continuous cause for celebration year after year, even though customs and traditions may change.

* **Listen to international Christmas music,** and dance joyfully in worship to our King. Celebrate the diversity of tribes and languages of all who join together to proclaim the joy of Jesus' birth. Find an international playlist at unwrappingthenames.com.

* **Cheer when you drive by nativity displays in town**, helping you remember the true reason for this Christmas season. You may even write out a note to thank them and place it in their mailbox. Find Christmas cards and more ideas at unwrappingthenames.com.

* **Watch a movie about the nativity of Jesus** and ponder which of His names are represented in the film. Then discuss together what stood out to you this year that you may not have noticed before.

* **Take cookies to your children's ministry leader or Sunday school teacher**, thanking them for sharing the Bread of Life with the children of the church.

BONUS CONTENT

Go to unwrappingthenames.com to download a free printable activity sheet and other fun resources to celebrate Advent together with your family.

WEEK FOUR

LOVE

This is love: not that we loved God,
but that he loved us and sent his Son
as an atoning sacrifice for our sins.

1 JOHN 4:10

LOVE

*I*f you are going through this devotional with your family, you can go to unwrappingthenames.com and print out the questions and Scripture readings on separate slips of paper and distribute them among your family members in order to involve everyone. Most of these components are simple enough for even small children to read alone or with help.

OPEN IN PRAYER

LIGHT THE FIRST FOUR CANDLES ON YOUR ADVENT WREATH

READ THE FOLLOWING VERSE ALOUD:

> "The people walking in darkness have seen a great light; on those living in the land of deep darkness a light has dawned." — Isaiah 9:2

SOMEONE ASKS:

> Why do we light the fourth candle?

SOMEONE RESPONDS:

> The fourth candle reminds us that God demonstrated His love by sending His Son Jesus to be born in a

manger and suffer and die for our sins, so we may live forever with Him.

READ THE FOLLOWING VERSE ALOUD:
"For God so loved the world that he gave his one and only Son, that whoever believes in him shall not perish but have eternal life." — John 3:16

TAKE TURNS READING THROUGH THIS PART OF THE CHRISTMAS STORY:
Luke 2:8–20

DISCUSSION QUESTIONS

1. God could have wiped out all humans and started over, but He chose to sacrifice Jesus so He could rescue us. What does this tell us about God?

2. How does the birth of Jesus show us God's love?

3. In what ways can we allow God's love to pour out through us into the lives of others?

SING THE FOLLOWING CAROL TOGETHER:
Away in a Manger

As you read your daily devotions this week, light four candles and thank Jesus for being our Love.

JESUS IS THE

GOOD SHEPHERD

I am the good shepherd.
The good shepherd lays down his life for the sheep.

JOHN 10:11

Some of the metaphors and examples Jesus used in His teaching can be hard for us to understand, though they would have made complete sense to Jesus' first hearers. Jesus as the Good Shepherd is one such metaphor. When He refers to Himself as the Good Shepherd, His listeners would have pictured a shabbily dressed, possibly smelly man who went all-out for his flock. A shepherd was dedicated to his sheep both personally and professionally; the sheep were his constant companions and his livelihood.

A good shepherd *cares* for his sheep: he finds pastures with lush green grass that will provide the nutrients they need to be healthy; he anoints their wounds with oil to foster quick healing; he protects them from the elements and from predators.

A good shepherd also *knows* his sheep: he nicknames them and knows their particularities; he watches them and knows if they're acting strangely or if they wander off; he provides for them individually exactly what they need as they age and develop.

A good shepherd *leads* his sheep: he goes before them; he walks the path before they do, making sure there are no dangers ahead; he always stays close to respond to any need that arises; he maintains a presence by whistling or singing so that they know he is always there.

Lots of hired shepherds would do those things too. An employee would have a vested interest in doing his job well. But the distinguishing mark of a good shepherd versus a hired shepherd is this: "the good shepherd *lays down his life* for his sheep." When danger comes, he doesn't run away to save his own life; he runs straight toward the menacing threat to attack it head-on, before it reaches his sheep. His own life is not worth saving if he loses his precious sheep.

That is our Good Shepherd. He doesn't have a superficial or halfhearted interest in us. No, Jesus is completely committed to us—caring for us, knowing us, leading us, and laying down His own life for us. Between continuing His existence without us and facing certain death, Jesus chose death. That's how much He loves us.

And that's the Good Shepherd who leads us. Be comforted by the reassuring presence of the Good Shepherd by your side.

CHALLENGE

If you're facing a menacing threat in your life right now, know that you are not alone. Though you may not see the Good Shepherd, He never leaves your side. As you go about your day, talk to Jesus and tell Him what you're facing. He knows you, cares for you, leads you, and will protect you with His own life.

PRAYER

Thank You, Jesus, for loving me even when, like a silly sheep, I run away. What a privilege it is to be part of Your flock, and to be known by You! Help me learn to imitate You in the way I love others, laying down my own desires to better serve those You've placed in my life. May my life point them to You, my Good Shepherd. Amen.

FOR FURTHER STUDY

Psalm 23; Matthew 2:6; Luke 15:1–7; John 10:1–18; Romans 8:31; 1 Peter 2:25

JESUS IS

IMMANUEL (GOD WITH US)

The virgin will conceive and give birth to a son,
and they will call him Immanuel, (which means "God with us").

MATTHEW 1:23

The verse above is the first of forty-three Messianic quotes from the Old Testament that Matthew included in his gospel narrative. By linking Jesus' life to the Old Testament promises, Matthew demonstrates that Jesus' birth and life fulfilled Old Testament prophecy, to show God's provision for His people and His faithfulness in following through.[1]

Jesus' birth and life physically manifest a spiritual reality: God wants to be with His people. He created humans with this relationship in mind, breathing His own life into us, creating us in His own image, and placing within us souls so we may commune with Him.

In the garden of Eden, God's presence was very real to Adam and Eve as He walked with them in the cool of the evening. Although Adam's and Eve's sin separated them from God, He was never far from His people. When He led the Israelites out of Egypt, He went before them in a pillar of cloud by day and a pillar of fire by night. His glory was visible in a cloud covering Mount Sinai, the tabernacle, and the temple as a manifestation of His presence.

Throughout history, God has demonstrated His longing to be close to His people. Sin has marred our relationship with Him, but Jesus' embodiment shows God's commitment to dwelling with His people.

This is mind-blowing when you think about it: God Himself set aside His brilliance, took on human form, and became one of us. He walked among us, ate, laughed, cried, slept, and felt tired, angry, happy. He, the Creator of the world, became as one of the created, because He longs to be with us. And He was willing to do whatever it took, even setting aside His glory, humbling Himself to the point of death—on a cross—just to be with us forever. Amazing love!

CHALLENGE

Today take time to respond to God's Immanuel by spending time in His presence, worshiping Him. Even if it's just two minutes, set aside your gift shopping, cookie baking, holiday frenzy and take a few moments to just be. With. Him. He longs for you and waits for you. Immanuel.

PRAYER

Immanuel, I'm so humbled by Your display of love! To think that You would willingly give up the glories of heaven to come to this lowly earth, to live with messy people, to die for ungrateful humanity, to secure for us an eternity with You. Forgive me for being so caught up in my own little life that I lose sight of that amazing love. Help me never to get over the amazement of what You did for me.

FOR FURTHER STUDY

Genesis 2; Exodus 13:21; 24:15–17; 1 Kings 8:10–13; Isaiah 7:14; John 1:14; Colossians 1:27

JESUS IS THE

SON OF MAN

For even the Son of Man did not come to be served,
but to serve, and to give his life as a ransom for many.

MARK 10:45

A close study of the Gospels reveals that the most common title Jesus used for Himself is "Son of Man." In fact, He used it eighty-one times in the Gospels though no one else used it to refer to Him.[2]

When the Jews heard Jesus call Himself the "Son of Man," their minds would have immediately leapt to Daniel 7. In this prophecy, Daniel writes about the end times, when "one like the Son of Man" will come with authority to judge the world. Jesus was claiming that title for Himself and communicating to His first hearers that He has the right to judge humanity.

But this title also refers to Jesus' own humanity. Think of the humility Jesus endured in becoming the Son of Man: God eternal and magnificent "made himself nothing by taking the very nature of a servant, being made in human likeness. And being found in appearance as a man, he humbled himself and became obedient to death—even death on a cross!" (Phil. 2:7–8).

Jesus emptied Himself of heavenly glory, while still retaining His deity, and submitted to the humiliation of becoming a human. From His position as Lord of the universe, He stooped down to become a servant, washing His disciples' dusty feet. He set aside all His prerogatives and became like one of us, bound by time and space, trading all the riches of heaven and becoming poor in both the literal and figurative sense.

This Son of Man was unlike any other son or daughter of man. Fully God and fully man, Jesus entered our physical existence and experienced the joys and anguishes of being human, yet without sin. What could possibly motivate Him to do this? Love.

That is the beauty of the doctrine of incarnation: God invisible, glorious, and untouchable took on flesh. For us.

CHALLENGE

In one of the most touching scenes in the Gospels, Jesus humbles Himself to wash His disciples' feet. Read John 13:3–17. Make a note of what Jesus knew going into this scene, how He responded to the different disciples (including Peter and Judas), and why He acted as He did. Jesus' example calls us to bow low in humble service. Who is God calling you to serve today? Imitate Him by stooping down and using your spiritual gifts to serve others as you would serve Christ Himself.

PRAYER

Jesus, Son of God, I'm so awed by Your life of humble service. You laid aside all glory and majesty to take on the form of a servant, while I grasp at the few strands of popularity and prestige I imagine I have. Forgive me, Lord, for the pride in my heart and my desire to be better than or more important than others. Make me a servant, and teach me to serve others joyfully.

FOR FURTHER STUDY

Daniel 7:13–14; John 13:3–17; 2 Corinthians 8:9; Philippians 2:5–11

JESUS WAS A

MAN OF SORROWS

He was despised and rejected by men,
a man of sorrows and acquainted with grief.

ISAIAH 53:3 (ESV)

In a society that avoids pain at all costs, Jesus' actions are hard to grasp. We're surrounded by medications to relieve pain. Many turn to drugs, abortion, or euthanasia in an effort to eliminate discomfort and inconveniences from life.

But rather than run away from pain, Jesus ran headlong into it.

In the garden of Gethsemane, we glimpse the mental anguish Jesus experienced before His betrayal. He told His disciples, "My soul is overwhelmed with sorrow to the point of death" (Matt. 26:38), and Luke describes Jesus' distress as so intense that His sweat was like drops of blood falling to the ground (22:44).

Knowing full well the suffering that awaited Him, Jesus pleaded with the Father to consider an alternative plan. The physical suffering He would have to endure alone would be enough to cause any one of us to turn away, and we now know enough about the Romans' cruelty during crucifixions to be shaken by their brutality. But Jesus also suffered the emotional agony of being forsaken by His Father, and the spiritual anguish of bearing all the ugly, inhumane, horrific sins of the world on His shoulders. It was enough to make anyone want to flee in the opposite direction.

But Jesus knew that there was no "plan B" to satisfy God's righteous wrath. Only He could secure salvation for His beloved creation, so He willingly accepted the hard road before Him even though He did not deserve any of it: the betrayal, the mock trial, the beating, the scorn, the humility, and the torturous death through suffocation on a cross.

Amazingly, Jesus had the power to stop it all with just one word, but His love for us compelled Him to step forward. He willingly walked into His suffering, humbly allowing Himself to be ridiculed by the very ones He came to save. Every agonizing moment He hung on that cross was another whispered "yes" to this painful course.

He who commands the universe and enjoys the worship of angels stepped down from heaven to be despised and rejected by humans. And He did it all for love.

CHALLENGE

For many, the Christmas season brings with it disappointment, loss, heartache, regret, and pain. We may lament and grieve what we don't have, even though we're surrounded by kitsch holiday displays and jolly season's greetings. Instead of ignoring this pain, allow it to surface and bring it to the feet of Jesus, who was Himself a Man of Sorrows, and understands the burdens that may weigh you down. There would be no joy if Jesus' story had not also included intense suffering and rejection. Today, meditate on Jesus' agony during His last moments on earth (John 18–19). Reflect on the fact that He knew fully what awaited Him at the cross but still submitted to the Father's will. Then spend the rest of your day worshiping Him, who was a Man of Sorrows and is now exalted at God's right hand.

PRAYER

O Lord, what can I say in the face of such love? The punishment that brought me peace fell upon You, and You willingly leaned into the suffering meant for me. Every sorrow and suffering I face, You faced first, and bore the wrath of God for me. Thank You, precious Jesus. Thank You.

FOR FURTHER STUDY

Psalm 69:29; Isaiah 53; John 10:17–18

JESUS IS THE

LAMB OF GOD

Behold, the Lamb of God,
who takes away the sin of the world!

JOHN 1:29 (ESV)

For most of Jesus' disciples, the word "lamb" would have conjured images of bloody sacrifices brought to the temple. But let's take a step back. Why would God require sacrifices in the first place?

Sin requires punishment and atonement. The sacrificial system was instituted by God Himself to satisfy His righteous wrath, turning it from those who deserve it to the object being sacrificed. Think of the first sacrifice recorded in Scripture: God slaughtered an animal to clothe Adam and Eve, covering them and their sins at the animal's expense.

We find many significant sacrifices in the Old Testament. When God tested Abraham's love, calling him to sacrifice his own son, Isaac, Abraham assured his son that "God himself will provide the lamb for the burnt offering" (Gen. 22:8). And God did provide: the ram Abraham found at the top of the mountain was killed instead of Isaac. This episode foreshadowed God's provision thousands of years later through the sacrifice of Jesus.

Another momentous sacrifice was the Passover lamb. After nine horrendous plagues sent upon the Egyptians in order to secure the Israelites' freedom, God sent a final one, meant to kill each firstborn son. But to protect the Israelites, God instructed them to sacrifice a lamb and brush its blood on their doorposts: "The blood will be a sign . . . when I see the blood, I will pass over you" (Ex. 12:13). Here, the Passover lamb points toward Jesus, whose blood would cause God's wrath to pass over those covered by it.

Throughout the Bible, sacrificial lambs were killed in order to bear the burden of people's sins. Sin was transferred from the guilty party to the animal. The person was declared innocent while the animal bore sin's just punishment: death.

This sacrificial system, instituted by God Himself, was limited in scope: the sacrifice of atonement was required every year. But it was all meant to foreshadow Jesus. The Lamb of God came to fulfill and supersede the sacrificial system. His death on the cross atoned for all of humankind's sins once and for all, through faith in Him.

This is not blind forgiveness but violent justice, not cheap grace but costly grace, not temporary oversight but eternal reconciliation. God doesn't ignore our sins; He acknowledges them and makes provision for them through His own Son. The Lamb of God makes possible our relationship with God.

CHALLENGE

Have you lost the wonder and awe of Jesus' sacrifice for your sins? Today, worship Jesus for His sacrificial atonement, for taking your sins on Himself. Pick a hymn or a song that speaks of His sacrifice, and sing it to Him in thankfulness. (See www.onethingalone/songs-of-worship for recommended playlists.)

PRAYER

Jesus, how can I ever thank You for taking my sins away? I deserve the wrath of God, but You bore that punishment and gave me Your righteousness. Take my life and let it be consecrated to You alone.

FOR FURTHER STUDY

Isaiah 53; John 1:29; 1 Corinthians 5:7; Romans 3:25–26; Revelation 13:8; 17:14

LOVE IN ACTION

*T*he activities below range from fun-filled family activities to service-oriented projects that you can do with your children or by yourself. Pick an activity from the suggested list below to put your love into action this week.

* **Write a letter to each of your children recounting a special Christmas memory.** Describe the scene in vivid detail, sharing what they were wearing, what smells were in the air, who else was there, and how you felt. Even if you don't consider yourself a writer, allow love to lace your words together.

* **Host a free pancake breakfast for international students**, playing gospel-centered Christmas songs in the background and asking them to share what Christmas is like in their home country. Look for opportunities to build bridges and point them to Immanuel—God with us.

* **Bake a birthday cake for Jesus**, the Son of Man, who left the splendor of heaven to take on human flesh. Encourage your children to think of ways they

might say "Happy Birthday" to Jesus by showing love to someone around them.

* **Have a hot (chocolate) date with your spouse** to reconnect and rekindle the romance in the midst of this busy season. Celebrate what's going well, and look for opportunities to affirm them and speak words of love over their life.

* **Tape $1 in quarters on washers in a laundromat** to serve those who may be going through hardship. As you do, pray that Jesus, the Man of Sorrows, would make His presence known to them through your simple act of kindness, and that they would feel part of their own burden lifted.

* **Set up a hot cocoa stand for the homeless** in your car or van and drive around the city handing out cups of warmth and words of love. Wish them a Merry Christmas, and remind them that Jesus, our Good Shepherd, sees them and loves them.

* **Shovel a neighbor's driveway or do some unexpected yard work**, praying for them as you work. If they join you outside, ask them to share their own favorite Christmas memories and traditions. Consider

sharing what you've learned through your readings in this Advent devotional, and look for opportunities to speak the truth of Jesus' love into their lives.

BONUS CONTENT

Go to unwrappingthenames.com to download a free printable activity sheet and other fun resources to celebrate Advent together with your family.

CHRISTMAS

*Today in the town of David a Savior has been
born to you; he is the Messiah, the Lord.*

LUKE 2:11

ʸᵒᵘ ʳ ᶜᴱᴸᴱᴮᴿᴬᵀᴵᴼₙ

ᴼ ᶠ

Christmas Day

I f you are going through this devotional with your family, you can go to unwrappingthenames.com and print out the questions and Scripture readings on separate slips of paper and distribute them among your family members in order to involve everyone. Most of these components are simple enough for even small children to read alone or with help.

OPEN IN PRAYER

LIGHT ALL FIVE CANDLES ON YOUR ADVENT WREATH

READ THE FOLLOWING VERSE ALOUD:

> "For God, who said, 'Let light shine out of darkness,'
> made his light shine in our hearts to give us the light
> of the knowledge of God's glory displayed in the face
> of Christ." — 2 Corinthians 4:6

SOMEONE ASKS:

> Why do we light the fifth candle?

SOMEONE RESPONDS:

> The fifth candle shows us that the waiting is over.
> Jesus Christ, the Messiah, is born!

READ THE FOLLOWING VERSE ALOUD:

> "The Word became flesh and made his dwelling among us."
> — John 1:14

TAKE TURNS READING THROUGH THIS PART OF THE CHRISTMAS STORY:

> Luke 2:1–40

DISCUSSION QUESTIONS

1. The eternal God entered this world as a baby in a manger, as a Gift for all people: rich and poor, educated and unschooled, young and old. What does this tell us about God?

2. How can we respond to God's great gift?

SING THE FOLLOWING CAROL TOGETHER:

> Hark! The Herald Angels Sing

NEXT STEPS

If you've grown closer to Jesus these last four weeks as you've journeyed through *Unwrapping the Names of Jesus*, you may be wondering, *What now? Where do I go from here?*

First of all, I'd encourage you to spend time reflecting on your relationship with Jesus: What have you learned about Him over the past few weeks? About yourself? About worship? Ask yourself, "Is God leading me to a specific action or change in my life as a result of this study?" Ask God, "Where do You want me to go from here?" God promises that when we draw near to Him, He will draw near to us (James 4:8). What a wonderful promise!

Secondly, I encourage you to connect with others in your local church and look for ways to serve and grow. You're also welcome to join myOneThingAlone, an online community of women who love Jesus and grow deeper with Him together through daily devotions and spiritual disciplines. Find more information and join us at www.myonethingalone.com.

Lastly, I would love for you to share this book with someone you know who needs to read it. Write a short post on social media with your honest thoughts, or leave a review online. That will help other people find this book, and I know they'll appreciate your feedback (and I would too!). You can also email me your thoughts at asheritah@onethingalone.com and let me know what your favorite name of Jesus has been from this study and how my team and I can pray for you. I look forward to reading your emails!

Joyfully serving the King,

Asheritah

ACKNOWLEDGMENTS

A book like this doesn't just happen overnight. Where to start in thanking those who made this book possible? I can't possibly remember everyone or say all that should be said, but I'll certainly try.

Thanks to Ingrid, Connor, Ashley, and the entire Moody Publishers team who saw the potential in this Advent devotional and helped prepare it for publication. What a joy it is to partner with you in your mission to resource the church's work of discipling all people!

Thanks to Pastor Mike, who read an early draft and helped me communicate what I really meant to say. You were so gentle and kind in your feedback, much like a shepherd watching his flock. Thank you for going above and beyond.

Thanks to Vicki, who jumped at the opportunity to proofread the first edition of this book and turn it around within 24 hours. I don't even want to imagine the horrors had you not lent your expertise to the shaping of this book. I owe you cookies. Lots of them.

Thanks to The Chapel family and my prayer team who have supported me throughout this process, from the self-published edition to this reprint with Moody and to all the books to come. You are my people.

Thanks to Kate and the #fmfparty community. You ladies are amazing. Seriously. I would have given up blogging and writing long ago if it weren't for your sweet fellowship and encouragement every Thursday night. When I pitter-pattered the keyboard to make words become devotionals, you all were on my mind. This book is for all of you.

And of course, I am always indebted to my family for their love, prayer, and patience with me as I ducked family commitments and scrambled back to my writing desk. To Eugen and Eli: you took a real interest in my writing projects and cheered me on even as we used to egg each other on growing up. I'm so lucky to be your sister!

Thanks to Mom, who has always been the biggest fan of my writing. She believed in my blog from its tiniest beginnings, and she tirelessly shares my writing with anyone who listens. Mom, you saw a little budding artist in me years ago, and you always told me I would write a book. Thanks for believing in me.

Thanks to Dad, who taught me to think critically and to question everything. He's given me a love for theology and a desire to dig deeper. Dad, this book would not have happened had it not been for your influence on my life. Thank you.

Thanks to Bunu Gabi and Buni Ica, who provided such gentle and loving care for my girls while I tapped away at the computer. I don't tell you enough just how grateful I am that you're in our lives.

Thanks to Carissa and Amelia, who see the best and worst in me and love me anyway. Precious ones, God has amazing things planned for you, and I'm so blessed to be part of your journey as your mama. May the good news of Jesus' birth impel love in your lives for His glory.

Thanks to my darling husband, Flaviu, without whom this book would have never grown outside the recesses of my heart. You recognized potential where I was afraid to even speak it, and you carefully tended to my dream like it was your own. You created pockets of time so I could write and poured yourself into nurturing my gifts. You. Are. Wonderful. *Te iubesc.*

And Savior, where would I be without You? All I am, all I have, and all I ever hope to be flows out of You so I can give back to You. Thank You for leaving the glories of heaven to redeem us as Your bride so we can spend eternity with You, unwrapping layer upon layer of Your glory. I can't wait.

NOTES

WHY CELEBRATE ADVENT?

1. Jonathan Bennett and David Bennett, "What Is The Season of Advent?," http://www.churchyear.net/advent.html; Dennis Bratcher, "The Season of Advent Anticipation and Hope," https://web.archive.org/web/20100202013406/http://www.cresourcei.org:80/cyadvent.html.

2. Philip Meade, "Four Reasons Baptists Should Celebrate Advent," *PhilipMeade.com*, November 26, 2011, http://www.philipmeade.com/uncategorized/four-reasons-baptists-should-celebrate-advent/.

3. Jen Wilkin, *Women of the Word: How to Study the Bible with Both Our Hearts and Our Minds* (Wheaton, IL: Crossway, 2014), 31.

4. To learn more about how to receive God's free gift of salvation offered in Jesus Christ, go to www.onethingalone.com/salvation.

WEEK 1: HOPE

1. R. C. Sproul, "The Resurrection and the Life?" *Jesus.org*, www.jesus.org/is-jesus-god/names-of-jesus/the-resurrection-and-the-life.html.

2. John Piper, "I Am the Light of the World," *Desiring God*, March 12, 2011, www.desiringgod.org/messages/i-am-the-light-of-the-world.

3. James A. Kelhoffer and John McRay, "Jesus Christ, Name and Titles of," in *Baker's Evangelical Dictionary of Biblical Theology*, ed. Walter A. Elwell (Grand Rapids: Baker Book House, 1996), 407–8.

WEEK 2: PREPARATION

1. "Word," *Merriam-Webster.com*, www.merriam-webster.com/dictionary/word.

2. Martin Vincent, "In the Beginning Was the (logos) ... (John 1:1)," *The Meaning of 'Logos' in the Prologue of John's Gospel*, January 1, 1887, www.bible-researcher.com/logos.html.

3. Randy Alcorn, "How Is Jesus 'the Truth'?" *Jesus.org*, www.jesus.org/is-jesus-god/names-of-jesus/how-is-jesus-the-truth.html.

4. C. S. Lewis, *The Lion, the Witch, and the Wardrobe* (London: Geoffrey Blessing, 1950; repr. New York: HarperTrophy, 2000), 80.

5. Mike Castelli, "Isaiah: Time to Choose" (sermon, The Chapel – Green, Uniontown, Ohio, May 7, 2017).

6. Richard L. Strauss, "The Holy One," The Joy of Knowing God series, *Bible.org*, https://bible.org/seriespage/holy-one.

WEEK 3: JOY

1. Ray Pritchard, "Great High Priest," *Crosswalk.com*, March 18, 2011, www.crosswalk.com/blogs/dr-ray-pritchard/great-high-priest.html.

2. Ibid.

WEEK 4: LOVE

1. Trent C. Butler, entry for "Old Testament Quotations in the New Testament," *Holman Bible Dictionary* (Nashville: B&H Publishing Group, 1991), www.studylight.org/dictionaries/hbd/view.cgi?n=4699.

2. John Piper, "Why Is Jesus Called 'Son of Man'?" *Desiring God*, April 4, 2008, www.desiringgod.org/interviews/why-is-jesus-called-son-of-man.

CONNECT WITH
THE AUTHOR

Connect with Asheritah and sign up for announcements and up-coming titles:

www.onethingalone.com

- * free downloads
- * blog
- * speaking events
- * membership community
- * and more!

Follow Asheritah on Facebook, Instagram, and Twitter:

@asheritah

one thing alone
FINDING JOY IN JESUS

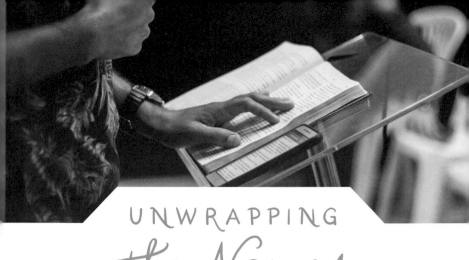

UNWRAPPING
the Names
OF
Jesus

ADVENT
CHURCH KIT

unwrappingthenames.com/kit

Kit includes a sermon series outline,
Sunday school curriculum,
Advent audio readings, and more!

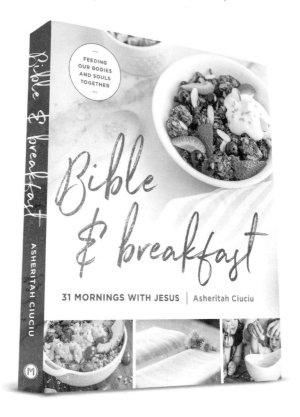

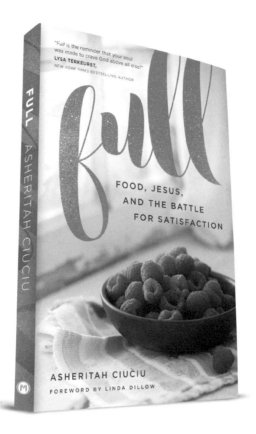

RELEASING JANUARY 2020

A
LENTEN
Devotional

UNCOVERING
the love
OF
Jesus

This Easter, experience God in a new way.